Poems for Today, Yesterday and Tomorrow

The Streets of my Mind

I0107933

G.J. O'Leary

U K Book Publishing.com

Design, typesetting and publishing by UK Book Publishing

www.ukbookpublishing.com

ISBN: 978-1-916572-82-9

Contents

THOUGHTS, IDEAS AND BELIEFS 1

Streets Of My Mind 2

A Leaf Upon A Tree 4

The Fish And The Bird 5

Questions 7

The Telescope 10

Sunday 12

A Simple Way Of Life 14

The Housewife 16

The Modern Home 18

Walk On Water 20

The Time Machine 22

The Time Machine 24

The Moon The Stars 26

Long Ago 27

The Dead of Night 29

Space and Time 31

I Am The Wind 32

Here And Now 33

CONTENTS

HISTORY 35

Ten Sixty Six (1066) 36

Summer 1981 46

Hillsborough 1989 47

Diana 51

CONFLICT 53

Private Charles Baxter 54

20th. Century 56

9/11 (Just Another Day) 60

The Terrorist. 2017 64

Prince Andrew 2021 66

The Queen's Jubilee 2022 68

Champions League Final 2022 70

POLITICS 73

Men 74

When The Circus Comes To Town 76

Brexit Rap 78

Climate Change 80

What Is It We live For 82

Shame 84

LEARNING 85

The Ant 86

The Selfish Body 88

Ocean 89

The Cockroach and The Beetle 90

Learning From Animals 91

Talking 92

The Sari 93

CONTENTS

Boys 94

Bullies 95

A Friend 96

Knowing 97

RELIGIOUS (SORT OF) **99**

Born To Know 100

It Matters Not 101

Born a Human Being 102

I Have No Name 103

Religion 104

Heaven and Earth 105

The Peaceful Prophet 106

We Are One 107

The Sinner 108

The Soul 109

The Book 110

Just For Today 112

A Basic Need 113

In-between 115

Life 116

Consciousness 117

Ridiculous 118

This World We Live In 119

Within and Without 120

What Part of Me is 'Me' 121

THIS AND THAT **123**

The Adults of Tomorrow 124

I See Not 125

Moments 127

CONTENTS

Aloneness 128

Who Am I 129

A Brightness and a Hum 130

Don't Get Upset 133

Two Worlds 134

Story 135

The Early Morning Bus 136

Winter Sunrise 140

Inner Self 141

Man of the Future 142

The River 144

PERSONAL AFFAIRS **147**

Great Dunmow 148

Mother B 150

Aigburth 152

Autumn 155

Retirement 156

A Family Holiday 158

Provence 160

Little Arrow 161

One In A Million 162

Brown Eyed Girl 164

Young Fair Child 166

I am There 167

Years 168

The Fifties 170

Thoughts, Ideas and Beliefs

Streets Of My Mind

The city is a busy and a bustling place
Where peace is so hard to find,
There's a corner I know where sometimes I go,
And it's on the streets of my mind.

And when I go there I stand and I stare
And watch all the people pass by,
Then I think of the time when I was a child,
How I wished like the birds I could fly.

And my dad would say,
"Son, if that's what you want
Then first you must learn to be kind,
Learn to love never hate, be patient and wait
And learn 'bout the streets of your mind."

And my dad, he knew, 'bout the streets of the world
In the night when the sun has gone down,
About the gambling dens, the drink, drugs and men
And the girls who walk around the town.

From a young boy I grew and what helped me pull through,
Were his words and that look in his eye,
The smile on his face, his warmth, his embrace,
If you want to you really can fly.

'Cause as I walk along I can hear the sad song
Of those people down there on the ground,
Yet the victims I see pose no problem to me,
Like a bird, I'm above all that sound.

And my body feels light as I walk through the night
Passed the noise from the bars of ill kind,
And if you take my hand on the corner we'll stand
And I'll show you the streets of your mind.

A Leaf Upon A Tree

In Autumn, walking through the park one day,
One hour before the dark,
I stopped beside an old oak tree
And wondered how it came to be.

Where do leaves go in the fall?
How from a seed does a tree get born?
Its shape, its colour, beauty, size,
A simple sight for simple eyes.

The roots embedded underground
And though it lives the only sound (I hear)
Are the rustling leaves,
As the wind blows around.

I walked on and thought some more,
Many times I've thought before,
This tree was here before my birth
Growing, outward from the earth,

And when my life I cease to live,
The tree lives on and life it gives
To other leaves in other Springs
And birds will nest and rest their wings.

And all the leaves just come and go
With Springtime sun and Winter snow.
Dare I compare my life to be,
Just like a leaf upon a tree.

The Fish And The Bird

To be free like a fish
That swims in the sea,
To be free like a bird
That flies through the air.

To be in one place,
At one time, to be free
To become what you are,
To be conscious, aware,

Of beginning and end,
Of here and now,
Of the meaning of freedom,
To know this, to know how.

To be free of this chain
Which is tied to the ground,
It's links made of currency,
Dollars and pounds

And not to be tied
By love or by hate,
But to do as needs must
And to leave more to fate.

To be free yet still loving,
Peaceful and kind
And to leave this connection
With ego behind.

To be free of the yearning
For knowledge and wealth
And not be afraid
Of old age or ill health.

To be free of frustration,
Anger and fear,
To hold close to the heart
All that which is dear.

To be free is the question
And the answer? I've heard,
Is to be your true self
Like a fish or a bird.

Questions

"What is Nature?"
The young boy asked the old man,
(Who was lying in his bed),
"Nature, means giving birth
And life on Earth", The old man said,
"And all the stars, what is or was or will be."

"Will you speak to me of science sir?"
The young boy spoke again,
"And where did mankind come from,
Please sir can you explain?"

The old man smiled and drew a breath
(Now feeling very weak)
And in a peaceful, distant voice,
These words the man did speak,

"Science be the questions asked
About the wind and rain,
About the trees, the sky, the sea
And life, from life was where we came."

Deep in thought the young boy sat
In silence in his chair,
And then he put this question
To his old friend laying there,

"Can you tell me of religion sir
Before you go to sleep?
There seems to be a diversity
Of religions and beliefs."

The old man looked intently
Into his student's eye,
He paused a while and then he gave
The novice this reply,

"Tradition is the garment
That religion tends to wear,
Many coats in many colours
So religion isn't bare,

Beneath this cloth of custom
Is where the spirit reigns,
Beyond the strings of mundane things
And hedonistic brains.

Your life, is your religion,
Your body is your church
And when your mind has come of age,
Your spirit will emerge."

Once more the boy was pensive,
The old man closed his eyes,
Gave out a sigh and left a smile
And then commenced to rise.

The boy, alone in silence
With the body of his friend,
Never noticed his departure
But this was not the end.

For though the man had gone away,
Had left and shed his skin,
A part of him stayed with the boy
Thereafter, deep within.

The Telescope

I once looked through a telescope
One clear and starlit night,
And I was filled with faith and hope
At this awe inspiring sight.

I saw the rings of Saturn
And the craters on the moon,
The sky took on a pattern
That starlit night in June.

I pondered for a moment
Upon the stars so high,
And wished that I could reach one
And among them maybe fly.

The stars are all so far away
And yet I still can see,
That within the night there shines the day
And up among those stars are we.

Perhaps if I could travel
At the speed of light,
I might then unravel
The significance flight,

For every little movement
Is an aspect of that speed,
Even my own heartbeat
Is a facet of the seed.

Perhaps then all I need to do
Is think and I'll be there,
Traveling through the universe
On this planet we call Earth.

For no matter where one is in space
The stars are there to see,
No matter what the time or place
Up among those stars are we.

Sunday

(A Moment of Bliss)

There's a horse chewing grass
In the field by the canal-side,
And a man with his dog
He's got a stick he's going to throw.

There's a barge sailing by.
Some swans are on the water,
A sparrow in the bird bath,
Time is passing slow.

There's a man with a line,
As he casts into the water,
There's a heron on the bank
Who wants that fish as well.

Some ducks are being fed,
The dog has got the stick now,
The heron's got the fish,
I can hear the chapel bell.

I want to wash the car
And I need to mow the lawn,
Maybe paint the fence
Or start some D.I.Y.

There's a jogger on the footpath
Another sparrow in the birdbath,
I take a sip of coffee
Some geese are flying by.

There's a lady in the kitchen
The smell of bacon frying,
She smiles and then suggests,
That we go out for a drive.

I finish off my sandwich,
take another sip of coffee
Pat the dog, the sun is shining,
It's great to be alive.

A Simple Way Of Life

We got supersonic, sub atomic,
Space flights to the moon,
With trips to Mars and far off stars
On the cards real soon.
We got laser beams, and now it seems
The sky is full of holes.
We got micro chips, cruise liner ships,
And hand held mobile phones.
We got microscopic, electronic,
Gadgets by the score,
We got satellites and cheap air flights
And junk mail through the door.
We got audio, we got video,
We got broadband internet,
Flat T.V. sets and online bets,
There's nothing we can't get.
We got 'round the clock news updates,
T.V. channels by the ton,
We got plastic, we got concrete,
We got oil and we got fun.
We got production lines of every kind
Of car in which to ride,
We got cameras on street corners,
We got nowhere we can hide.
We got debit cards and credit cards
A luxurious life of debt,
We don't think about tomorrow
'Cause tomorrow ain't here yet.
We got nuclear reactors,

Pollution in the air,
We got over-population
We got greed and we got fear.
We got computers, we got cyberspace
And holidays in the sun,
We got G.M. crops and sales in shops,
Black Fridays, two for one.
We got climate change and forecasts range
From scorching to ice cold,
We got winds that splice and melting ice,
Our Co2 we're told.
We got hedonism, terrorism,
We feed on all the hype,
What we got no more and that's for sure -
A simple way of life.

The Housewife

Six a.m. breakfast in an hour,
Lay the table, then a shower.
Get the kids all off to school,
"Please behave don't act the fool"
Leave the house and lock the door,
Come back, clean, and brush the floor.
Go the shops, select the food,
No time to think or laugh or brood.
Bring home shopping, put away,
What's the weather like today?
Do the wash and hang it out,
Check the files, the bank account.
Kettle on, make a cup,
Do the dishes, the washing up.
Tend the garden, grass needs cutting,
Check appointments up and coming.
Grab some lunch, a bite to eat,
No time to take weight off her feet.
Forgot the fuel for the car,
Never mind it's not that far.
On the road back to the shops,
All red lights, all these stops.
Back home again now running late,
That call to friend will have to wait.
Cut the grass, clothes are dry,
Iron and fold and love apply.
Make sure to tidy up the home,
Collect the mail, answer the phone.
Change the bedding, move that stool,

Pick the kids up from their school.
Think of what to eat tonight,
Cook the dinner, make sure it's right.
Help with homework, time ticks on,
" Tell me where has this day gone."
Hubby home, make his meal,
Slice the carrots, potatoes peel.
Feed the kids, "Now where are they"?
All gone missing outside at play.
Call their names, get them in,
She'll close her ears to the din.
Sit down together, begin to eat
At last some weight is off her feet.
Talk about events today,
Listen to what they have to say.
Clear the table, don't mind me,
They're watching football on T.V..
"How many times now have I said?
Come on children off to bed."
Run the bath, make sure they clean
Their teeth and say just what I mean.
Put out clean clothes, and clear away,
Tidy up once more today.
Look at the clock it's time for bed,
Time to rest her sleepy head.
"Think I'll shower in the morn"
Not long now before the dawn.
Dreams of comfort, time for me,
Dreams of sun and sand and sea,
Enjoying friends and family time,
Nibbling cheese and drinking wine.

The Modern Home

Machines to wash dishes,
Machines to wash clothes,
Vacuum cleaners and driers
And DAB radios.
Pumped in electric,
Water and gas,
Lighting and windows
With two panes of glass.
Living room lounges
With comfortable chairs,
Wardrobes and cupboards
And under the stairs,
For hanging our coats and placing our shoes
And household utensils
We don't often use.
There's duvets and curtains
And carpeted floors,
Central heating, hot water
And lockable doors.
Driveways and gardens
And garages too.
Bedrooms and bathrooms,
Showers and loos.
A car, a computer, a flat T.V. set, Music on hi fi,
Broadband internet.
Kitchens with ovens,
Fridges and freezers,
Draws holding scissors,
Nail file and tweezers.

Knives and forks,
Dishes and pans,
Spatulas, spoons,
Food stored in cans.
A dining room table
Complete with its seating,
Where the family can gather Together when eating.
And taken for granted
The home we adorn,
Be gracious and thankful,
We don't know we're born.

Walk On Water

Walk on water, float on air,
Free your self from stress and fear.
Transcend your being through time and space,
Feel the magic of its embrace.

Lying down upon the floor
Free your mind from every chore,
Breathe in deeply then exhale,
Think not of size or weight or scale.

Think not of heaven nor of hell
For this is you, alive and well.
Chant a mantra say a prayer
Feel that sense of everywhere.

Imagine mountains high above,
A lake serene, the sense of love.
Rise up now beyond the sky,
Beyond the hills begin to fly.

Expand your mind, get release,
Feel that sense of inner peace.
Walk on water, float on air,
Search your being for self lies there.

See the rose, the scent of flowers,
While away the time, the hours,
Touch the edge of all sublime,
Think not 'me', nor " I'or mine.

Spend sometime alone each day
Search for your peace in a simple way.
Walk on water, float on air,
Now open your eyes -
You're already there.

The Time Machine

Part One

A man stepped into his Time Machine
And closed the door behind,
Then travelled back to a time before
The birth of all mankind.

He came to rest on a mountain ledge
And surveyed the land below,
Valleys, forests, in all shades of green
And mountains topped with snow.

He roamed the rivers and the lakes,
Pausing by some waterfalls,
He listened to the thunder
And the voice of Nature call.

He sailed the deep blue oceans,
Passed the ice caps on the way.
The desert sands, the canyons and
All this in just a day.

And it all looked so familiar,
So too the setting sun,
So too the crescent moon,
Time travel changes none.

Then in the night, shining bright
Against a pitch black sky,
A trillion stars shone from afar
In wait of mankind's eye.

He watched the sunrise from a cliff
Aside the morning song
Of birds and breeze and Earth at peace,
Before man came along.

A man stepped into his time machine
And closed the door behind,
Returning to the present day
With another voyage in mind.

He wondered how the world would look
Two thousand years from now,
Would man have laid the Earth to waste,
And took his final bow?

Would he have ended conflict
Or settled one last score?
Would he have pressed that button
And have fought his final war?

The Time Machine

Part Two

A man stepped into his Time Machine
And closed the door behind,
Then travelled to the future,
To see what he could find.

To a time when man had ceased to be,
Had vanished in the mist,
Where all man-made machinery
No longer did exist,

No Cities, towns or villages,
Just forest, grass and glades,
In fact no sign of anything
That man had ever made.

No sight of roads, no paths or tracks,
Each building turned to sand,
All what man had taken
Had returned back to the land.

But what he saw like the time before
Was an awe-inspiring scene,
Rivers, lakes and mountains,
Wildlife, running free.

Blue lagoons and coral reefs,
Shores of sun-drenched golden sand,
Vegetation, fruit and vine,
Untouched by human hand.

No toxic waste, a clear blue sky,
A fragrant atmosphere,
No other place in all of space
With which one could compare.

This planet Earth, this garden,
Nature has it here to give,
This island in a Cosmic sea,
A perfect place to live.

The Moon The Stars

The moon, the stars,
The rising sun,
The Earth, the past,
The times to come,
The trees, the grass,
The morning dew,
Flowers, meadows,
Me and you.
Fish of the sea,
Birds of the air,
Insects, plants,
Life everywhere.
Animals wild,
Like wolves and bears,
Best left alone,
Dare not go near.
But dogs and horses
Lend us a hand,
Animal friends
At man's command.
The sky, the clouds,
The wind and rain,
The rivers and mountains,
The desert plains,
The ocean blue,
The beach, the sand,
None of this made
By mankind's hand.

Long Ago

If we lived some time ago
More than three hundred years,
What work would we be doing?
How more (or less), would be our cares.

For there would be no factories
For building motor cars,
There would be no rocket ships
Blasting off to Mars.

There would be no aeroplanes
Flying overhead,
No diesel locomotives,
But sailing ships instead.

No package tours or coach trips
Taking folk away,
To places which seem distant,
Yet not so far today.

Cobbled stones and unlit streets,
Wood to fuel the fire,
Worn out clothes and hand-me-downs
Would be the norm attire.

No super stores for shopping in
Few comforts in the home,
No T.V. sets, computers,
No fridges, telephones.

Yet the labours of the past
(Removed from life today),
Kept us closer to the land
And to the light of day.

For technology and science,
Never will replace,
That connection with the natural world,
With timelessness and grace.

The Dead of Night

When silence descends on the City at night,
When the noise has settled down,
When the pubs and clubs have locked their doors
And deserted be the town.

When the dark early hours are here once more,
When the revelry has ceased,
Shadows play their little tricks
When empty are the streets.

Alleyways and back cracks
Devoid of sound and light,
Not a place to wander
Within the dead of night.

A drunkard walking oddly
Along the street alone,
He's spent all of his money
And he's missed the last bus home.

The roads now bare of traffic,
Of pedestrians and light,
The mess that's left behind,
Is not a pretty sight.

Pavements strewn with litter,
With thrown away kebabs,
Takeaways and burger buns,
Chicken legs and fags.

Shadows and odd noises
Threaten, causing stress,
Street cleaners in the distance
Busy cleaning up the mess.

Then as the dawning light returns,
Work beckons them again,
Race and rush and traffic jams,
How monotonous the game.

This game of work then merriment,
Seeing not, beyond their youth,
Seeing not a life worth more than this,
Living falsehood, not the truth.

Space and Time

Just one time,
Just one space,
Just one "here"
Just one place.
Just one "me"
Just one "you"
Just one day
With lots to do.
Just one "now"
Just one light,
Just one world
In wait of night.
Just one love
To help one cope,
Just one dream,
Just one hope.
Just one space,
Just one time,
All mine is yours,
All yours is mine.

I Am The Wind

I am the wind and the rain,
I am the rivers and the ocean,
I am the mountains and the valleys,
The meadows and the trees,
I am the flowers and the grass.
I am of earth and of flesh,
But more than this, I look on,
In awe of these.

Here And Now

Here is the place
Where the past is no more,
Now is the time
When the future is born.

This is the moment
That forever has been,
This is the time
One awakes from the dream.

The Earth in the heavens,
With the Sun and the sky,
No need to question
Or even ask why.

With crops from the soil
And water from rain,
No hunger, no thirst,
No need to complain.

Fish from the ocean
Fruit from the vine,
Bees making honey
As if by design.

Heat from the fire,
Shelter from storms,
Thoughts to inspire,
Clothes to keep warm.

Air, beauty and colour
Completely surrounds,
Mystery and magic
Forever abounds.

Nothing too near,
Nothing too far,
The moon in the night sky,
Millions of stars.

The dawn chorus of birdsong,
Flowers and trees,
An abundance of life form
Non greater than thee.

No clocks and no time
From the moment your born,
Only the seasons,
The dusk and the dawn.

A place to discover,
The world at your feet.
With beautiful people
To grow with and meet.

A place to have children
And no child should miss,
The here and the now
In this moment of bliss.

History

Ten Sixty Six (1066)

Saxons

Ten sixty six
We all know what happened,
William The Conquerer
Saw off King Harold.

At the battle of Hastings
They all heard him cry,
He got hit by an arrow,
Went straight through his eye.

The Saxons were finished,
The Normans took over
And poor old King Harold
Put to rest in the clover.

Normans

So William the First
Of Normandy fame,
On Christmas Day in Westminster
King of England became.

Then in ten eighty seven
William died all alone,
So his son, known as Rufus
Took up the throne.

And Rufus became
King William part two
And he wasn't well liked
Between me and you.

While out on a horse-ride,
The story went 'round,
He got struck by an arrow
And fell dead on the ground

In the year eleven hundred
For his brother they called
And Henry the First
To the throne was installed.

So Henry the first
As king did survive,
From eleven times a hundred
To eleven three five.

After he, not his daughter, Matilda,
Not a woman for Queen!
So they chose cousin Stephen
With the related gene.

Plantagenet

Then Matilda's son Henry
Of Plantagenet corps,
Took up the mantle
In eleven five four.

He was Henry the second,
Then Richard the first
The Lionheart King,
Crusades and battles and that sort of thing.

Then in eleven ninety nine
King John, to rule had a thirst.
His barons revolted
With a grievance they nursed.

King John got surrounded
At old Runnymede
Magna Carta was founded,
A charter agreed

In twelve sixteen
Came Henry the child,
He was Harry the third,
Stayed around quite a while.

In twelve seven two
Came Edward the first,
The hammer of the Scots,
For their blood was his thirst.

Thirteen and seven,
Edward Two came to be,
Then Edward the third and
Richard the second finished that dynasty.

Lancaster

The Lancastrian House
Thirteen ninety nine,
Took up the mantle of
King For a time.

With Henry the fourth
And two more with that name,
Henry the fifth
Of Agincourt fame.

And Henry the sixth
In fourteen twenty two
Took the crown as a child,
A storm started to brew.

York

The wars of the Roses
Brought violence and tears,
Twixt Lancaster and York
Lasted thirty two years.

Edward the fourth
Then his brother the fifth,
Uncle Richard the third
And a long standing myth.

Tudor

After which, house of Tudor
On the scene came alive.
With Henry the seventh
Fourteen eighty five.

Next, Henry the eighth
No need to explain,
In fifteen and nine
To the throne the man came.

And of his six wives
Only one did survive,
Two lost their heads
Two divorced and one died.

Edward the sixth
At the age of nine,
In fifteen forty seven
Was king for a time.

Then bloody Queen Mary
In fifteen fifty three,
Put to death all protesters
Who didn't agree.

Enter Elizabeth the first
In fifteen five eight,
Sorted out Mary Stuart
Then at the Spanish Armada,
She through all her weight.

Stuart

In sixteen and three
Tudor came to an end,
The House then of Stuart,
To the Crown did ascend.

With King James the first
(Mary's son) was a Scot,
Then his son Charles the first,
Then the Parliament lot.

The Parlis beat Charlie
In a long civil war,
Charles was beheaded
So he was no more.

Republic

Sixteen forty nine
Olly Crom' took the helm,
So the head of the army
Ruled over the realm.

He ruled as protector
'Till they all changed their mind,
Replaced by King James
Of a catholic mind.

Stuart

For Mary, his daughter,
A Dutch husband was arranged,
From The House-of Orange
Inducing much change.

At the battle of Boyne
They all had a fight,
The protesters won
And James took to flight.

So a King and a Queen
On the throne came to be,
Mary the second
And King Billy three.

In seventeen and two
Ascended Queen Anne,
No heir did she leave
So the Germans began.

Hanover

Hanoverian rule
Their Dynasty name,
For a century and more
They took up the reign.

Twas seventeen fourteen
When they came to the fore,
The first of The Georges,
One, two, three and four.

In Eighteen and thirty
William Four got crowned,
For seven short years
He was around.

Saxe Coburg Gotha

So ascended the throne
The long serving Queen Vic.,
For sixty four years
She carried the stick.

Saxe, Coburg, Gotha,
Was Victoria's house,
She ruled over an empire
With Albert, her spouse.

Then Bertie the Seventh
'Till nineteen and ten,
His son George the Fifth
Took up it he then.

Windsor

And during world war
George changed the name,
To the House of Windsor
The family became.

Nineteen thirty six
Edward the Seventh,
(Who soon abdicated),
He ran off with a woman
And both got berated.

So it came to non other
Than Edward's young brother,
Who had an affliction
An embarrassing stutter.

All through World War Two
Did George the Sixth reign,
'Till Elizabeth the Second
To England's throne came.

One nine five two,
George suddenly died,
The following year
Elizabeth arrived,

At Westminster Abbey
To be crowned England's Queen,
And televised World wide,
A spectacular scene.

And she's proved so far
Serving the longest,
Held it together,
Some say she's the strongest.

In the twenty first century
The Royal family still stand,
Prince Charles in the wings
Waits, the crown of the land.

In two thousand twenty two,
Died Queen Lilly Bet.,
Now her son Charles the Third
Crowned the oldest king yet.

Over one thousand years
Have passed this land by,
And a history of monarchs,
No man, can deny.

Summer 1981

Now we are together,
Now we are united,
Prince Charles has married Lady Di
And made us all delighted.
The country celebrated
With parties in the street,
There was joy and there was happiness,
The world was at their feet.
And all the noble dignitaries
Came from far and wide,
Kings and Queens and Heads of State,
To see the blushing bride.
The joyous celebration
Went on all through the day,
They dined until they had their fill
Then went upon their way.
Yet as the night befell them,
Amid the peace and quiet,
A cry rang out from Toxteth, Brixton, Solihul,
Oh yeah, it was just another riot.

Hillsborough 1989

The fifteenth day of April,
Nineteen eighty nine.
A football semi final,
The F.A. Cup this time.

At three pm the whistle blew,
The match had just begun,
The players were oblivious
Of the horror that had come.

The police were there in force,
The commander lost the plot
When he gave that fatal order,
An order he should not.

An overcrowded Leppings Lane
Where the victims met their fate,
Crushed against the fences,
When opened was the gate.

No deployment of the barriers
To direct the eager fans,
And of accountability
All would wash their hands.

For as the gate was opened
Crowds outside began to rush,
Overcrowding now much greater,
So much greater now the crush.

At three 'o' six the whistle blew
The ref had stopped the game,
People being crushed against
The fence in Leppings Lane.

Daughters, sons, and husbands
Who earlier bright and fresh,
Could not breathe and could not move
Against, a steel erected mesh.

Fences on the terraces,
What for and what to stop?
Now thousands more had filled the lane
And the fans began to drop.

With no sense of a disaster
High command began to rot,
Only Bobbies without instruction
(And fans, with make-do stretchers)
Was all the dying got.

Just one lone ambulance
Was kept outside at bay,
And why? No-one would answer,
No authority would say.

And mud would sling, with news reports,
Crowd disturbance, so it read,
"A ticketless, tanked-up drunken mob"
Robbing from the dead.

Politicians, judicial inquiry,
Newspapers, especially one,
The corridors of power,
Laying blame on those fans who had gone.

Seven and ninety lost their lives,
A whole city shed its tears,
Yet for the truth to be exposed
It took so many years.

A football match, that's all it was
Where fathers had gone with their sons,
Where daughters, and brothers and sisters,
Would never return to their mums.

Months after this needless tragedy,
The fences were withdrawn,
And so, all seater stadia
At the grounds became the norm.

The years just kept on passing by,
Yet compassion, love and giving,
To the fighting families of those who died,
From the grieving, thankful living.

For seven and twenty years
The truth they had concealed,
False statements and a cover-up,
But justice now, was sealed.

A long time for some people
Of responsibility and power,
To be exposed, for what they were,
A corrupt, dishonest, lying shower.

The twenty sixth of April
Two thousand and sixteen.
Outside the courts of justice,
A victorious, tearful scene.

The jury had concluded
The verdict (unlawful killing) had been reached,
No, the fans were not to blame,
The Law, The Police, had breached.

Justice for the ninety seven,
In our hearts came some release,
Prayers for the souls who lost their lives
May they now all rest in peace.

Diana

It's reported in the papers
That there's trouble with the Royals,
Prince Charles has got a mistress
While Diana's blood just boils.

So she got herself a playboy
And is doing her own thing,
While Charles and his Camilla
Make plans for when he's king.

As Diana's out in Paris,
With her Dodi in a car,
They're speeding through the city
But they don't get very far.

While the paparazzi chase them,
Their driver just sees red,
They crash inside a tunnel
Now poor Diana's dead.

CONFLICT

Private Charles Baxter

(In the battle for Zonnebeke, Flanders WW1 Sept 1917)

Death awaited in Flanders
On the battlefields of war.
Blood, detached limbs,
Thousands of bodies lay dead on the floor.

Royal powers reigned over
Both the rich and the poor,
Stubborn pride of world leaders
Had to settle a score.

Some wanted a bigger
Slice of the cake,
Some, just sworn enemies
Out on the make.

They recruited young soldiers
To fight and to kill,
To bleed and to die,
To go over the hill.

To stand in the way
Of cannon and mortar,
To fight in trench warfare,
Become part of the slaughter.

Thousands were buried in the earth
Where they fell,
In the mud, in the blood,
In that man made hell.

High ranking orders
From the officer corps
And Private Charles Baxter,
Came home no more.

20th. Century

One hundred years have come and gone,
Extremes of poverty and wealth began
A century, and n'er before on such a scale
Did change occur on history's trail.

Low pay, no dole, no pension pot,
No N.H.S. the poor man got.
Votes for women, suffragettes,
Empires on the verge of threat.

Oil, (black gold) the west did find,
Took up arms, but all were blind
To the pain and shame that was to come,
Like at the battle of The Somme.

For a great world war descended down,
Blood, and millions dead
Lay on the ground.

Over oceans, across the land,
Modern ways unleashed,
Via telegraph and radio
The Western word was preached.

The roaring twenties had their day,
Rich and famous all at play
And while the rich were spending cash
It vanished with the Wall Street crash.

The third decade left its mark,
Jobs were scarce, the future dark.
Then war once more came to be,
The holocaust atrocity.

Flying warheads, atomic bomb,
Hiroshima, Nagasaki ----gone.
Fifty years at last some peace,
Restart, rebuild and youth unleash.

The swinging sixties, Vietnam,
Immigration, colour ban.
Fashion, pop and T.V. sets,
A wall between the East and West.

The Cuban crisis, C.N.D.
It nearly happened - world war three.
Propaganda, you can pay
Tomorrow, for your greed today.

Music, art, no more gloom,
Men are walking on the moon.
Media moguls, celebrity,
It's in the papers, on T.V.

The seventies draws the line,
The price of oil they redefine.
Assassination, terrorists,
The Middle East strives to exist.

Eighty years have passed in time,
Technology is near its prime.
The working class have got enough,
The business world starts getting tough.

Micro-chips and silicone,
In the office, in the home.
The dawn of electronic age,
Prudence, wisdom, take backstage.

The Berlin Wall is no more,
A new world order at the door.
And as the nineties come to be,
The Western world in luxury,

On your marks, get ready, set,
The coming of the internet.
Space Shuttles and mobile phones,
Test-tube babies, ovine clones.

Motorways and cities crammed,
With motorcars in traffic jams.
Retail stores packed with goods,
Hurricanes, wide-spread floods.

Melting ice caps, Co_2,
Global warming, what to do?
The ozone layer wearing thin,
Far fewer men now seek within.

Rising crime fuelled by the need
For drugs and sex, booze and greed.
And as morality declines,
Above us all the sun still shines.

Not by bread alone we live,
The source of Man has more to give.
Love and hope, still felt by some,
Begins the third millennium.

9/11 (Just Another Day)

To the global world of finance
It was just another day,
Yet it ended all in rubble,
In smoke and dust and clay.

Like thunderbolts from hell,
Flying through the sky,
At ground level watched in silence
By disbelieving passers by.

The aeroplanes were carrying
Those who had no say,
To them another plane ride
It was just another day.

While observers caught on camera,
Could not believe their eyes,
And transmitted 'round the globe
What was happening in the sky.

And we all remember where we were
On that morning nine eleven,
Etched into all our memories,
That terror from the heavens.

Still we ask the questions
In whose name and as to why,
Such inhuman acts of horror
And still yet no reply.

Those inside the towers
In air conditioned rooms,
Just watched it through the windows,
Their fast approaching doom.

No time to run or panic,
No time to hope or pray,
But stay frozen to the spot
On just another day.

On ground level in a moment
Time stood still or so it seemed,
As they hit, shouts of,
"Oh my God"
The horror and the screams.

And The Pentagon fell silent
As they listened to the roar
Of what seemed to be a missile,
Come crashing through the door.

It was just another day
When a high pitched awesome sound,
One more jet just nose dived
Then exploded on the ground.

And those who planned and did it
Can not be understood,
How in the name of God
What they did they believed was good.

The Towers were a symbol
Of finance and of trade,
A place of global business,
On this stage the scene was played.

On upper floors those who were trapped
By smoke and fumes and heat,
Chose to jump out through the windows
To their death into the street.

They'd gone to work that morning
And to the towers made their way,
Had said farewell to loved ones,
It was just another day.

And brave fireman to the rescue
Leaving coffee on the hob,
Clambered up the stairways,
It was all part of their job.

But to watch those towers come crashing down,
Though true it felt unreal,
Like a huge disaster movie,
It all seemed so surreal.

And one's feelings of sheer terror
And of grief, one could not hide,
To think of all those people
Who by fate were trapped inside.

Who had gone to work that morning
While the sun was shining bright
And were all part of three thousand,
Who were mourned that very night.

Yet since that fateful morning
No man can ever say,
That tomorrow when it comes,
Will be just another day.

The Terrorist. 2017

So you think it's really worth it
To go into a rage
And sacrifice your given life
For a moment of rampage.

And you believe you are a hero
For God or for your faith,
So you fill your heart with anger,
With violence and with hate.

Then you arm yourself with weapons
Or don your deadly vest,
You really believe you're different
And more worthy than the rest.

So you plan to die a martyr,
Do you really think that's wise?
To die and take them with you,
The innocent you despise.

There's something you should think about,
We all die in the end
But most of us live out our lives
With family and friends.

And though life's tribulations
Sometimes drive us to despair,
We have each of us to lean on,
We have love and those who care.

So we live and work and laugh and play
And together we grow old,
All else is just a mind-set
And stories we are told.

We have no hate or jihad,
No belief that needs to score,
So why not come and join us
And pledge to kill no more.

Prince Andrew 2021

Prince Andrew's been taken off duties,
His title and status has changed,
Was accused, playing games with a minor,
He denied it was him, but it's strange.

Photographed with an acquaintance,
Who was imprisoned for serious crime,
In his house in New York where it happened,
And who goes by the name of Epstein.

The public where shocked to discover,
Guislain Maxwell was guilty as well,
Then choke marks were found 'round Geoff's neck line,
They found him, dead in his cell.

Virginia had said in her statement
In a nightclub was where she first met
The Prince, who was sweating profusely
The worse dancer that she'd ever met.

This doesn't sit well with Royal Families,
The Prince went on camera and said,
"I wasn't there, on day in question,
Took my daughters for pizzas instead."

As far as it goes in the nightclub,
He denies it was he that she met,
He has a medical condition
That causes him never to sweat.

To prevent being summoned he decided
To pay compensation and fees,
Go public and beg that they listen,
Requests that his story gets believed.

So then Her second son Andrew
Was told by his mother, The Queen,
Will no longer be called His Royal Highness,
Such scandal,
The whole thing's obscene.

The Queen's Jubilee 2022

Queen Elizabeth the Second of England,
On the throne for seventy years,
Through happiness, through heartache,
Joy and fun and tears.
Through good times and through bad
She carried the nation through,
From one era to another,
She's been there for me and you.
From steam railways through to motorways,
From triumph to disaster,
From analogue to micro chip,
She's been the nation's master.
She travelled 'round the world
On her journeys to promote
The best of being British,
By 'plane and train and boat.
She's seen the coming and the going
Of Prime Ministers, fourteen,
And Presidents of the U.S.A.
So far the same amount she's seen.
Her annus horribilis
In ninety ninety two,
She suffered most intently
Yet still came shining through.
She's answered all the questions
By the silence she's maintained,
Standing out alone
As Head of State she has reigned.
Through war and epidemic,

Through strife and through unrest,
Since nineteen fifty two she's reigned
And strived to do her best.
Queen Elizabeth, Britain's Monarch,
We all can safely say
Steadfast, resolute and stoic,
Has she been since her crowning day.
So let us join together
As we come to celebrate,
The platinum jubilee
Of Elizabeth the Great.

Champions League Final 2022

How inhuman, how subversive,
How cruel can power get,
When sent to order crowd control,
Law and order is the threat.

When families come together
To cheer on and to support
Their football team, the players,
The police authority resort -

To cruelty and to violence,
To maintain and keep the peace
Of the joyous and the peaceful
As they gather in the street.

Using batons, using tear gas,
To disperse with pepper spray,
Families herded all together,
Put in danger, in harms way.

Creating victims from the crushing
And the pushing of the crowd,
While the gangs of local thugs,
Rob the unsuspecting proud.

Proud women and proud children
Proud men who've come to celebrate
A champions football final,
All made to stand and wait.

And funnelled through the turnstiles
Like cattle to the slaughter,
Young and old, men and boys,
Brother, son, sister, daughter.

This behaviour, this corruption,
From authority, the law.
From police and from security
These crimes the fans endure.

When will they ever understand
This passion and its meaning ?
The coming of togetherness
Turned into all this grieving.

It's competition, it's just rivalry
It's not street gangs dressed in red,
It's supporters, it's the fan base,
Who's hard earned wages they have shed.

It's scandalous, it's disgraceful,
You're the cause, you are the blame,
They called themselves a police force ?
They should hang down their heads in shame.

Politics

Men

'Twas men who made our laws, (long ago)
And men who go to war,
And men who invade other people's shores.

'Twas men who sailed the seas, (long ago)
In vessels carved from trees
And men, who gave names to all of these.

Is it nought but men
Who've wrought,
Through the content of their thought
The type of world that men deem it to be?

Big egos and ideas (of men)
And like minded peers,
Are these the cause
Of inequality ?

I fear It's men who are to blame
For the torment and the pain,
That they've brought upon us all
Through history.

And the vanity and shame,
That's upon us all again,
Is it not the fault of men,
This tragedy?

Yet if men could just be men
And not boys or ego's toys
And were with Mother Nature to comply,

They would walk with heads held high,
With their women by their side
And live peacefully together
By and by.

For men are Kings,
But are they worth their Queens
Or the fruits passed up by Earth,
Could they not destroy us all without a trace ?

With their bullets and their bombs,
Has not the time now come
(for each and every one),
To pray for men
To save the Human Race ?

When The Circus Comes To Town

When the politicians gather,
Broadcast in sight and sound,
The cameras have a field day
When the circus comes to town.

The reporters and the journalists
All clamour, gather 'round,
As they tell us of the breaking news
When the circus comes to town.

There's Donald Trump and Putin,
And our P.M. Theresa May,
There's Macron, Merkel, Juncker,
All report and have their say.

Kim Jong-un from North Korea
With his missiles underground,
All leaders of their nations,
But it's the circus come to town.

And it's just the same old stories
With different faces that astound
It's all so disingenuous,
When the circus comes to town.

The clamour to report the news
Seems to mask the truth I've found,
The ring-master is the media
It's the circus come to town.

And we watch them on our TV sets,
The internet abounds
And we don't know who to believe no more,
When the circus comes to town.

Brexit Rap

They thought that they could fix it
By advocating Brexit,
So Cameron took the biscuit?
With Eurosceptics tried to mix it.

He called a referendum
And we listened to the humdrum
Of the tiresome and the wearisome
Of this political conundrum.

His way of trying to shut them up,
He thought that he could cut them up,
They forced his hand and roughed him up
And in the end he mucked it up.

It all backfired, it came about,
The Leave campaign had the loudest shout,
In voters' minds came Euro doubt,
It was left to the people and they voted out.

Now we're left in a right old mix up,
Cameron's gone, it's a right old stitch up,
Milliband, Clegg, Farage, all fixed up.
Boris got dropped and Corbyn cocked up.
May's in charge it's just a mock up
Division, no vision, they should all be - locked up. ——

More than two years up the line
Nothings clearer so we're told
No one knows how it will unfold
Theresa May is looking old.

So are we in or are we out?
Do we get another shout ?
Is there anyone there with a bit of clout?
Will another election come about?

Is there anyone there who understands?
Is there anyone there who can lend a hand?
I only hope it will turn out grand
Was this really what they planned?

Climate Change

The destructive force of nature
Reigns down from up above,
On all those things we come to cherish,
Unknowing, come to love.

And when the wind has come
With the power of sea and rain
And floods the roads and dwellings,
Which we must build again,

When lives are lost and properties
No longer do exist,
And all that's left there in its wake,
In the silence and the mist,

Is abject devastation
Which we never did expect,
From the wings of such as butterflies,
El Niño the effect.

Earthquakes and tsunamis,
Nature's fury surely looms,
Forest fires surrounding cities,
Tornados and typhoons.

But live we must in dangerous times,
Through weather so extreme
As climate change brings hurricanes
And awakes us from our dream.

Power stations and oil platforms,
Fossil fuels burnt by the ton,
The motor trade and modern lives
Close our ears to Nature's hum.

Rain forests disappearing,
In place of all the trees,
A concrete world of CO2
Burning oil and C F Cs

Havoc thus created,
The future lies unknown,
Climate change and melting ice
The making, much our own.

So the modern world's real legacy,
The harm already done.
Is the progress, man believes he leaves
To generations yet to come.

What Is It We live For

What is it we live for?
Celebrity and fame?
Designer clothes, fast cars and stuff?
To play the spending game?

What is it we're here for?
To be winners big and strong?
To demand our rights, what's mine is mine,
Put right that which is wrong?

What sort of life is this we live,
From who's image do we carve ?
What is it we live for?
To consume? get rich or starve?

To envy those from Hollywood
In their jewellery, pearls and gold?
With their face lifts and their tummy tucks,
To hide the fact their growing old.

Should we not be building character,
Inner strength and self respect,
Modesty and honesty?
Worthy of our intellect.

Should we not be teaching dignity
To help our children in their plight ?
Show them love and show them kindness,
Simple wrong from simple right?

For it's they who we pass on this world,
And they who'll come to be,
The owners and the tenants
Of the sham and drudgery.

And they will be the bankers
Politicians and MP's,
Law makers and the parents of
Generations yet to be.

Do we tell them of the pitfalls?
Know how to keep them safe from harm.
Is this not what we live for?
To foster peace and grace and calm.

Shame

Over indulgence, over feed,
We stuff ourselves
With pride and greed.
We take, we break,
Destroy, we steal,
Beneath our feet
We fail to feel,
This tender Earth
From which we came,
And Human life
We put to shame,
With guns and bombs
And violent tongue,
Ever warlike
And think we strong.
When there are those
Who have no bread,
Who are half starved
Or underfed.
Who walk the land
With naked feet,
While all the rest
Eat market meat
We dress ourselves
In designer clothes,
Without much thought
For such as those,
Who live their lives on charity
And wish like us,
That they could be.

Learning

The Ant

An ant stepped onto a blade of grass
And then onto a twig,
She climbed upon a squirrel
And did a little jig.

After that she climbed a cat,
She scaled a dog and then a horse,
She sprang onto its rider,
Who knocked her off of course.

She landed on a mud heap,
Right by a giant tree
And up the trunk the ant did go
To a higher place to see.

She climbed upon a nightingale
And soared up to the sky,
High above the treetops
She watched the clouds go by.

She found herself a night owl,
Saw the moon lit by the sun
And wondered what had stirred in her
And what had just begun.

The sight of all those stars above,
The galaxies and space
And she a simple insect
In this living, breathing, place.

Returning to her day job,
Back amongst the earth,
She rejoined her blissful colony
With no sense of self or worth.

But she was happy with her family
And content with being scant,
Playing with her friends all day,
Such a busy little ant.

The Selfish Body

Five parts of the body,
One day went to war,
Over which part worked the hardest
Who performed most of the chores.
"It's me who works the hardest," said the legs.
"I take all the weight, I carry us around all day
And run when we are late."
"Not you that works the hardest," said the arms,
"For where would we all be?
Who'd wash and cook and carry
If not it were for me?"
"Your wrong," then said the body,
"I'm the most hard working part,
I contain all vital organs, like the kidneys, Lungs and heart.
"Enough of this complaining," said the head,
"There's something you have missed,
Can no one see the truth?
It's as one that we exist."
"Each one of us contributes,
I show us all the way,
Together we accomplish,
Each has their role to play."
"I think and hope and I believe
And I cry out in despair,
When I hear you disagree like this, It's not kind or just or fair."
"We are all one in one body,
To each from each we give
Nature works in unison,
There's no other way to live."

Ocean

Where did the ocean come from ?
It was there before fish in the sea.
Where did the ocean come from?
It's a question that's puzzling me.
Did it fall from the sky in a rainstorm,
Filling the craters below ?
If so then how did the clouds form,
Can anyone say that they know?
And where did the mountains rise up from,
Or the sand on the beach and the trees,
Can anyone say how this happened ?
Can someone explain to me please.
So how did the soil on the ground form,
With its worms, flowers and plants
And who made the beetles and spiders,
All the insects, the bees and the ants?
So where did the ocean first come from
All the fish and the life forms I see
And where did the people all come from ?
Not forgetting of course little me.

The Cockroach and The Beetle

The cockroach asked the beetle
To go out on a date,
"We could both go to the cinema,
We'd be there by half past eight."

"I'd rather walk the hedgerow"
The lady beetle said,
"Or perhaps play in a mud heap
Or this rock pile here, instead."

Cockroach -

"But it's warmer in a building
Amongst the dust and dirt,
Underneath the floorboards,
Far less chance of getting hurt."

Beetle-

"Oh no, I like the open space,
Where I feel so fresh and free,
That's the difference 'tween you 'roaches
And beetles just like me.

You are dirty and a health risk
And you spread bacteria too,
I'd rather date a beetle
Not a cockroach like you."

Learning From Animals

If you can stay silent In a noisy house,
When surrounded by bedlam
Stay quiet as a mouse.
If you can be different,
Unfazed like a cat
And remain unmoved
Upon meeting a rat.
If you can be stately
Like a black stallion horse,
Be proud, show no ego,
Be yourself of course.
If you, like a dog
Can stay faithful and true,
And be wise like an owl
So they can't corrupt you.
Then you my friend
Will live a good life,
You'll need nothing else
To cope with the strife.

Talking

Some people talk
Their few words say a lot,
Some people go on
That's all that they've got.
Some folk are quiet
Or don't say too much,
Some speak with a smile,
An embrace or a touch.
Some folk are kindly,
Use words that are sweet,
And some folk are harsh
And not so discreet.
Some people think
Before what they say,
And some folk just shout
And can't find their way.
There are those who are silent
Yet dwell in their heart,
You always can tell
These ones apart.
For they hold the secret
That words can't explain,
Deep down they're no different
For all are the same.

The Sari

The lady wore a sari
That covered to her feet,
For she rejects the fashion culture
Of those ladies down the street.
Who walk with off the shoulder dresses
And skirts that only seem to please,
The eyes of men who ogle
And want them higher than the knees.
No, she'd rather wear her sari
That stretches to her feet,
Which expresses the shear beauty
In her face, when all she greets.
So to emphasise her modesty
And the female form so sweet,
She prefers to wear her sari
That covers to her feet.
She doesn't want to tempt such men
With flirting stance nor tease,
Those who only want to touch
Or kiss or hold or squeeze.
So she wears her dresses modestly
And well below her knees.

Boys

Some boys stray and some boys pray,
Some are good, some bad.
Some protect and some take care
And some just wish they had.
Some boys try and some boys cry
And some boys lose their way,
Some boys win and some boys lose
Yet try another day.
Some are vain and some boys shame
Some are very proud,
Some are peaceful, some are not
And some just very loud.
Some are strong and some are weak
Some are in-between,
Some are loyal and some betray
Some cruel and some just mean.
Some are bright and some are wise
Some are clowns, some fools,
Some are cheats and some are fun
And some play by the rules.
All boys need encouragement
They have it in their blood,
Learning from their parents,
The meaning of what's good.

Bullies

Don't whimper in the corner,
Don't buckle at the knees,
Don't stamp your feet or gnash your teeth,
For bullies often tease.
Don't show them that your angry,
Show no fear nor show conceit,
Ignore that sense of butterflies,
Stay upright on your feet.
Look not away or downward,
To the side or to the sky,
Direct your gaze toward them,
Look them in the eye.
Let them have their moment,
Let them have their say,
Watch them from within yourself
And let the children play.

A Friend

A friend is such on who you rely,
A friend is such either girl or guy,
A friend is such who is there for you,
A friend is such who you're there for too.
A friend never queries ask what or why
A friend never will intrude or pry,
A friend is a shoulder to cry on, a crutch,
A friend will ask not of the other too much.
A friend is forgiving, who knows the real you,
A friend is uplifting when you're feeling blue.
A friend is one who will never compare,
A friend when in need, will always be there.

Knowing

There are those who know not,
(and will never know)
There are those who know not,
(but are learning)
There are those who know bits,
Go mad or take fits,
Or for power and wealth ever yearning.
There are those who know best,
Those who know more than the rest,
And those who are gentle and wise,
These and all those who know that they know,
Can see without using their eyes.

Religious (sort of)

Born To Know

We were born to be not savage,
Not to judge, to fight or kill,
We were born to get to know ourselves
And this we're doing still.

It Matters Not

It matters not I follow Christ
Or be a Muslim or a Jew,
It matters not that I be atheist,
Buddhist , or Hindu.
For we are all of human kind
Who have but just a day,
To breathe love and peace and kindness
Into these lumps of clay.
Made we from the stuff of stars,
From ashes and from dust,
And brought to life by a greater power,
Than any one of us.

Born a Human Being

I was born not a Christian
A gentile or a Jew,
I was not born religious
That gets bestowed on me and you.

I was born not an Irishman,
A welshman or a Scot,
I was born in Liverpool
So Scouse is what I got.

I was not born a rainbow
Neither yellow green or blue,
I was male and I was white
So I said, well that will do.

I was born a human being
A living breathing child,
All else got bestowed on me
To save me from the wild.

I Have No Name

I have no name
I cannot speak,
I have no knowledge
And no belief.
I have no hate
I have no greed,
Love and care
My only need.
I live, I breathe,
I'm undefiled
I am the infant,
New born child.
I am here,
I've come to be
And everyone,
Was once like me.

Religion

Is it something to escape to
With its rituals and prayer ?
That strives to help this troubled world
And keep in mind, God there.
Or is it like a window?
By which, it comes to pass,
While climbing through the framework
They get trapped inside the glass.
Far better then to seek and find,
Knock, and go out through the door,
For, (after looking through the window)
What they see, they can't ignore.

Heaven and Earth

The books have been written,
The words there to read,
The warnings been given,
Few ever take heed.
The prophets have spoken,
Their wisdom ignored,
Violence and malice,
The trend now adored.
The laws of our nature,
Have often been aired,
But virtue and goodness,
Seems no-one has cared.
When will we take notice?
When will we all learn?
For a place there in heaven
On Earth, must be earned.
The truth has been spoken
For what it is worth,
The doorway to peace
Is right here on Earth.

The Peaceful Prophet

A peaceful prophet, a Godly man
With a message to convey,
That mattered much in ancient times
And just as much today.
He spoke in parables and anecdotes,
With tales of rich and poor.
And told them all to seek, to ask
And knock upon the door.
They said he spoke in riddles
To explain the spirit's call,
Whisper to a few,
Or proclaim to one and all -
That no diamonds are in heaven,
There are no mansions in the sky,
As the camel that can never fit
Through a needle's eye.
They said The Heaven that he spoke of,
Fills hearts with love and grace.
The Heaven that's in each of us
Is not of this worldly place
He sought silence in the wilderness,
And solace in that too,
Forgiving those who did him wrong
"For they know not what they do"
Yet who's example do we take, ?
Who's ideas do we follow, ?
Today, in this the modern world,
Will it still be here tomorrow?

We Are One

She is one with the Earth,
When a woman gives birth,
We are one when we sing,
When happiness rings.
We are one when we grieve
And when we believe,
We are one when we share,
One when we care.
One when we give,
When we live and let live.
We are one when we die,
We are one bye and bye.

The Sinner

I confess I am a sinner,
I confess that I have strayed,
I confess my own wrong doings,
And the goodness I've betrayed.
And I pray for some forgiveness
To cleanse my soul and mind,
And I vow to walk an upright path
And the sinner, leave behind.

The Soul

I heard the soul is what makes us laugh,
It also makes us cry,
It's there at birth (and throughout our lives)
Then leaves us when we die.

The Book

Mathew, Mark, Luke and John
And Jesus Christ have been and gone.
They spoke of love, of peaceful ways,
Forgiveness, faith and hopeful days.

Spoke simple truths, some rules to keep,
As you sow, so shall you reap.
He blessed the poor, He blessed the weak,
Showed how to turn the other cheek.

He cured the sick and raised the dead,
Son of God so they said.
He turned their water into wine,
Years ago in Roman times.

Roman times of slavery, hedonism, civil war,
Corrupt officials, rotten core.
In the politics of ancient Rome
A world religion's seeds were sewn.

The Roman state in decline,
A Holy Empire commenced to shine.
Written down the story went,
Around the world the word was sent.

So came The Book in His name,
Contrite remorse, their tune had changed,
They wrapped themselves in religious chain.
That sordid world they rearranged,

Inspiring art and making way,
For Church and hymns and Godly day.
Yet meditation, simple prayer,
The Human soul got lost somewhere.

Century's passed, opposing beliefs,
Brought war and death, pain and grief.
Lessons learned from the past,
All forgotten, the die was cast.

Now we worship to our shame,
Credit, profit, wealth and fame.
The consumer world, the Godless State,
Corruption, crime, anger, hate.

And so the cycle carries on
Affecting each and everyone.
We think us not part of the chain,
In Karma's grasp we all remain.

We laugh, we sigh, we grieve, we weep
As we sow, so we reap.

Just For Today

Just for today
I'll be patient and say
Not a word if others complain.
Just for today I'll be mindful the way
I answer their needs and refrain ...

From being judgemental or quick to reply,
I won't get frustrated or down,
Just for today I'll smile, that's the way
To diffuse the moment, not frown.

Just for today
I wont show dismay
When others just wont let me be,
I'll show what I'm about, believe and not doubt,
Stay true to myself that's the key.

I'll show that I care and be more self aware
Of how I may look or appear,
I'll relax, get above with a sound sense of love,
Anxiety, frustration and fear.

Then when it's time, go to bed feeling fine,
Join hands and say a short prayer,
Be thankful for peace and my own cooling breeze
And say "Thanks" for just being there.

A Basic Need

When gone are the days of childhood,
Of games and nursery rhymes,
Of chocolate and of ice cream
And the bliss of childhood times.
When days of adolescence
Have been and had their day,
When the days and nights of manhood
Are here with us to stay,
Days of independence
And responsibility,
In a world of greed and selfishness
And cunning trickery,
Where all believe they're different
And yet look all the same,
Where violence and indecency
Are all part of the game.
Where happiness and peace of mind
Appear just out of reach,
Where wise men and philosophers
Have lost their power to teach.
Where capital and finance
Rule our destiny
And undermine our self respect
And our dignity.
Where they've made a God of business
And budget paranoia,
And of social care and welfare
Made a sacrificial fire.
Where science and technology

Dictate our beliefs and creed,
Neglecting, in our ignorance
Of just one basic need.
Rekindle days of childhood
And refresh the memory
With those days of trust and innocence,
That are there for all to see.
The basic need for all of us
Always will remain,
Within the seeds of childhood
And all that is Humane.
It's there for all to contemplate
It's there for all to see,
Look at the fresh born infant child
No closer could one be.

In-between

Chaos rules not the day,
For order is supreme.
So why is it they often say
There's nothing in-between ?

Life

Life the arena
Where consciousness grows,
What lies beyond
God only knows.

Consciousness

I cannot see with eyes the sight of it,
Or hear with ears, its sound,
I cannot know in wakefulness
Of that, which all surrounds.
I cannot smell or taste or touch
Or reason why its here,
And yet I know (through Consciousness)
Of consciousness,
Of this I am aware.

Ridiculous

I believe that it's preposterous
To say that we're alone,
No Godly light to guide us,
No heaven to call home.
I believe it's just plain ludicrous
To say it all began
From nothing,
Resulting in all life on Earth
And the consciousness of man.
Some say God is a fairytale
To forever keep alive,
Why do we need this belief in God
To help us all survive?
A fairytale? ridiculous !
And here's the reason why,
No God, no hope, no purpose
And nothing when we die.

This World We Live In

Some think it is a playground,
Some look on it with fear,
Some a place to scream and shout,
Some to laugh and cheer.
Some think it is a mountain
Uphill all the way,
Some class it as a punishment
For the wrongs they do or say..
Some believe it is a garden
To tend to with great care,
A place of wondrous beauty
To cherish and to share.
Some believe it is a classroom
And some a science lab,
Some a place to write about,
Some a place to brag.
Some think it's just a place to live,
Some a place to question why
And some a place to starve, to pain,
Get sick, get old and die.
Some believe this world we live in
Is what Mankind has wrought
And some believe it's all of these,
Some, nothing of the sort.

Within and Without

Ask your self this question
Answer if you dare,
If you looked inside yourself
What would you find there?

Would you find contentment
Or would you find distress,
Would you find resentment
Or peace and happiness?

And when you look out from within
What is it you see ?
The same or something different,
What difference could there be?

It's up to each, to me and you
To choose the peace which helps one cope,
To listen to ones inner self
With faith and love and hope.

What Part of Me is 'Me'

What part of me is me?
What part of you is you
For we are not the things we see,
Nor the things we do.

We are not the laughter
That we make when we are glad,
And we are not the tears we shed
When we're feeling sad.

We are not the places
Where we've been or going to,
Nor all the dreams that we may dream,
That do or don't come true.

We are not the guilt we feel
When we, have got things wrong
Or the anger or the hurt,
We're the singer, not the song.

We are not the mood swings
That we get from time to time,
That lift us up or put us down,
But something makes us shine.

We are not the beliefs we believe
Or the thoughts that we may think,
And our feelings are the waters
From the wells from which we drink.

But there is a part in all of us,
That part of me and you,
The part that says, "No that's not me"
The part we know is true.

This and That

The Adults of Tomorrow

The adults of tomorrow
Are the children of today,
They'll be our providers
When we are old and grey.
If we don't care for them with love,
If we don't treat them right,
Then what can we expect of them
In our a-ged plight.?
There are some age old people
Who look down on youth with shame,
They are their children's children,
Who else can they blame.?
So all parents of young children,
Must needs you to take heed,
It's your children who you'll turn to
In your later, greater need.

I See Not

I see not the plastic
The concrete and the steel,
I see not the polythene,
To me they have no real appeal.

I only see the mountains,
The flowers and the trees,
I only see the grasslands,
The woodland and the sea.

I see not the railway lines
The trains and boats and planes,
I see not the motor cars
That clog up traffic lanes.

I only see the sunshine,
The shining moon at night,
The stars and all the galaxies
Are a much more worthy sight.

I see not the office blocks
Rising up into the sky,
I only see the wildlife
And the birds as they fly by.

I see not the palaces,
The pavements and the streets,
I see not technology
But the world beneath our feet.

I see not the vanity,
The envy or the greed,
I only see humanity
And the love that we all need.

Moments

The most joyous moments in our lives
Are those closest to the heart,
Memories of good times gone by
From which we never part.
A handshake or a well wish
From family member or a friend,
A warm bed to climb into
Late at night, when at days end.
The chorus of the birdsong
As dawn begins to break,
The rumble of a nearby stream,
A country walk for walking sake.
A bright brisk winter morning,
A sunny holiday away,
A smile from a passing stranger,
Good morning so to say.
Simple moments passing by,
Moments we all share,
We rarely notice having them
Or attest to them being there.

Aloneness

Like the sun in the sky
Or the moon full and bright,
Like a cat on the prowl
Or a moth 'round a light.
Like an island surrounded by an ocean of blue,
Or a babe in the womb
That's anytime due.
Like a fisherman casting
His line with its bait,
The river is tranquil
And he patiently waits.
Like a jog in the rain
Or a crisp winter walk,
A stroll in the sunshine
No need for talk.
Like a desert oasis
Or a dog with a bone,
No, aloneness means not
Being Alone.

Who Am I

Who am I?
What is 'me'?
What is, my last identity?
For I am not a dreamer
Nor am I a dream.
I am not a fiction
Not what I'll be or what I've been.
I am not a character in a storybook or play,
I am not a fairytale,
I'm real as clear as day.
Standing by a river
And though it is the same,
Not the drop that's flowing past,
Each water drop has changed.
Call each drop a man or woman,
Brother, sister, son or daughter,
Passing through eternity
Just like this gushing water.
And standing here I ponder
As time goes passing by,
Ageing, changing, wondering,
Asking who am I?

A Brightness and a Hum

Before his birth, from a tiny cell
To a foetus in the womb,
And he could hear and move as well
Inside this small cocoon.

And all controlled by Nature,
Unborn and yet to feel,
Sight and sound and taste and touch
This world so very real.

Then as a new born babe in arms
Unknown to right or wrong,
He mostly slept sometimes he wept
For food to make him strong.

Consciousness unfolding,
A brightness and a hum,
Turned into sound and all around
Something had begun.

"I am not alone", he thought
And he began to see,
Shape and colour everywhere
And people "Just like me".

And so he learned to walk and talk
And run and jump and play,
And read and write and wrong from right
To help him on his way.

Then as a boy and life a toy
Told carefully to tread,
He learnt at school some golden rules,
With no thought for times ahead.

Kick balls, climb walls, cut knees from falls,
Play football in the street,
Play games with friends until days end
In the sunny summer heat.

Days out by the seaside,
The smell of fresh sea air,
And in the sand with his own hands
Build castles by the fair.

In his late teens a change of scene
For youth was fresh and wild,
He'd laugh and joke and drink and smoke
But still he was a child.

Then older still he met a girl
They fell in love and wed,
They made a home they called their own
With children to be bred.

And as their children grew,
The man now came to see,
The innocence of childhood
And what can and cannot be.

I guess he knew that as they grew
Their kids would leave one day,
The world revealed, they'd play the field,
Then each go on their way.

To raise families of their own,
With childhood tales to tell
And watch their children grow,
Then leave the family shell.

And grew he wise, as time passed by
Now leader of a clan,
Hard and slow, blow by blow,
A matured and seasoned man.

And then one day now old and grey,
His time had almost come,
He could see and hear, what babes hold dear,
A brightness and a hum.

Don't Get Upset

Don't get upset by the ways of the rest,
There's something much better to do
When they step out of line stay silent it's fine,
Remember the good that's in you.
Don't get upset by the ways of the rest,
When negative thoughts fail to cease
Don't get sucked in to their ways and their sins,
Think good and think silence and peace.
Don't get upset by the ways of the rest,
Seeming always to get their own way
By waiting your turn the good that you earn
Will bring you a huge sum one day.
Don't pay no heed to the gossip and greed
And the bad news reports on TV
Don't get sucked in by the shame and the sin
Believe in the good that you see
Don't think about time or 'me' and what's mine
For life is no race or a trend,
Empty your mind of thoughts of bad kind
And embrace your good nature my friend.

Two Worlds

Look beyond the body
To that which lives inside,
An innocent that's driven
By an outer, artificial tide.
Influenced and hypnotised
By celebrity and fame,
Blind to Mother Nature.
And all that is humane.
Made sightless by the concrete,
The plastic and the steel,
Controlled by time and finance,
Unborn, and yet to feel -
The freedom, of a bird in flight
Or a stallion on the plain,
A dolphin in the open sea,
A child, before it's named.
Modern minds enshrined in prejudice,
Drugged on sex and beer,
Stuck in the mud of greed
And in the sands of fear.
Behind these times of luxury
Mother Nature fully glows,
Two worlds and just one simple choice,
Which one to let go?

Story

How the drip, drip, drip, of a story
Can change the way we think,
How blind we are to this sad sad club,
How low we all can sink.
How easily we follow
The lead of such few men,
That one per cent of us all
And the power afforded them.
The porn, the drugs, the violence,
The constant news of vice,
The T.V. shows and cinema
That glorifies, incites.
How sad sad sad society,
The corruption and the sleaze
Afflicting young and old alike,
With that cold cold old disease.
How full of kindness is the cup,
How empty is the jar,
How easy good can pick one up
And show us who we are.

The Early Morning Bus

There's a postman standing at a bus stop,
It's cold at five A.M.
It's snowing and he's all wrapped up,
He's on the early shift again.

A lady stands behind him,
A cleaner, likewise on her way,
To clean a block of offices,
At the very start of day.

The bus approaches slowly,
Braking easy not to slide,
It's icy, people boarding
Find it's just as cold inside.

They smile and say good morning,
Now at last their on their way,
Having something small in common
Early, on a winter's day.

The snow has stuck with ice below,
It's dark and hard to see,
Bus heaters slowly warming,
De-misters clearing not the screen.

Out on the street, a vagrant,
In a doorway on the ground,
Rapped in slumber, rags and cardboard,
Never is he homeward bound.

Further on there's been a car crash,
It is not a pretty sight.
Police are there in attendance,
With their blue and flashing lights.

On the bus returning journey,
A man at bus stop stands alone,
He's finished work, been on the night shift,
Looking tired on journey home.

A window cleaner with his ladder
Has ventured out now snow has ceased,
A corner shop is selling papers
People start to fill the streets.

Comes alive the dawning city,
Out of slumber like a waking child,
And as the hours pass on by us,
Tranquil peace now something wild

It's the turn of office workers,
Must be at work by nine-o-clock,
Runners trying hard to catch it,
Just in time, get to the stop.

Production line and dockside workers,
Plumbers, joiners, from the building trade,
Car mechanics, electricians,
Carry snacks their wives have made.

Later on, queues get disruptive,
Children, kids, all off to school,
Some board showing good behaviour,
Some don't pay and play the fool.

Later still the weary pensioners,
Show there pass and sit they down,
A trolley, scarf, a coat and hat
Off to the shops, market, town.

Now mid morning getting busy
Heavy loading, traffic jams,
All the hustle and the bustle,
Shopping trolleys, mums and kids and kiddies prams.

Car horns honking in a hurry,
Many vehicles speeding by,
It's getting crowded pax are standing,
All the sound is amplified.

Crowds of fans on their way to
A football game, a big event,
Rushing, pushing, in a hurry,
Nothing here is heaven sent.

Department stores are filling up,
Another year another sale,
The town is hectic, thousands gathered,
Some healthy faces, most are pale.

Bus driver now has nearly finished,
Lunch and sleep coming soon,
Pay-in takings, take a catnap,
Overtime this afternoon.

Park the bus and hand it over,
Feeling hungry, need a meal.
Early shift is almost over,
The middle man now takes the wheel.

Winter Sunrise

It's dawn, the sun is rising,
A scene to you I bring,
Snow has fallen in the night
And covered everything.
The trees, the hills, the fields, the vales,
As far as one can see,
Nature shows her face, unfolding-Beauty, majesty.
And as the shadows of the dark
Give way unto the dawn,
The morning sun climbs higher,
And another day is born.
The snow is crisp, the air is fresh,
The sky above is blue,
And here we stand looking out
In wonder of the view.
Then the morning, comes alive
Embracing winter sport with thrills,
Children come from far and wide
Sledging down the snowy hills.
A playful interaction
(a thought for what it's worth),
The human correlation
Between us and Mother Earth.

Inner Self

All around in sight and sound,
Reflections of what's true,
For what you see in others
Is also there in you.
If we could see the chamber
Within which life is played,
And look inside with swallowed pride
To that soul which is enslaved,
Take a suckling child at feed-time,
Distant from all pain,
With warmth and love and nourishment,
Refreshed, reborn again.
With no inner chains of torment,
No prejudice inside,
At the centre of this very soul
True human self resides.

Man of the Future

He woke up one bright summer morning
But something just wasn't quite right,
All the people he knew had just disappeared,
They had vanished it seemed, overnight.

All of his aunties and uncles,
His siblings and cousins all gone,
His parents, old school friends and workmates,
No one around him, not one.

His wife had also gone missing,
His kids now had kids of their own,
As he entered the bathroom, in the mirror he saw,
A wrinkled old man, all alone.

Then later that bright summer morning,
He decided that he'd spend the day,
Visiting friends and his family,
To just pass the time and to say,

"Hi and how are you doing?
I was just passing by and you know,
I thought I'd call in to see how you are,
For a chat, and to just say hello."

He then made a date with his family,
To party on Saturday night,
He invited some workmates and neighbours,
For the time he believed, was just right.

He said to his wife on that morning,
That he loved her and that he was blessed,
To have such a wonderful family,
And with trivia no longer obsessed.

He then took his kids to the playground,
Had rides on the swings and the slide,
Had fun playing football and cricket,
They laughed so much that they cried.

He woke up the following morning,
And he looked in the mirror again,
He saw who he was, that young married man,
In appearance nothing had changed.

Had he seen himself in the future?
He knew not, but believed that he should,
Live out each day of the rest of his life,
In touch with family and friends while he could.

The River

Come gather round, I have a tale,
A story I must tell,
About the place where I was born
And knew and loved so well,

And though the river's running still
Away into the sea,
Upon its banks lay empty docks
Where tall ships used to be.

And in the town where I grew up
On streets of cobblestone,
Were taverns full of sailor men,
Singing shanty songs of home,

But now there's just tall office blocks
Where the taverns used to be,
And yet the river's running still,
Away into the sea.

Behind the old horse stables,
A marketplace stood there
And to the Village Green they'd come
To buy and sell their ware.

Where now a shopping precinct stands
And the Village Green has gone
And yet the river's running still,
Still flowing on and on.

In summertime we'd reap and sow
The fields of corn and wheat,
Now multi-storey car parks
Back alleyways and streets.

On Sunday morn' the church bell rang
From the chapel on the hill,
Now run busy traffic lanes
And the chapel bell lies still.

We'd sail the river every day
My young friend and I
And charge the folk a farthing each
To cross from side to side,

Today, two tunnels and a bridge span the one mile gap,
Taking them across the flow
And bringing others back.

I can no longer recognise
My birthplace anymore,
Except the flowing river
and some stops along the shore.

We dreamed of sailing oceans wide,
Me and my young mate,
But then one day our boat capsized,
And we met another fate.

Now it's time for me to go
I must take my leave,
Return back to my resting place,
Back to the sea to sleep.

For I was once a sailor-boy,
That's where I long to be,
Flowing with the river tide
Away into the sea.

Personal Affairs

Great Dunmow

Surrounded by rich farmland,
With meadows lush and green,
In winter, spring or autumn.
A picture postcard scene.

In the countryside of Essex
Lies this ancient market town,
Thatched cottages and coffee shops,
And for flitch trials is renowned.

There's the High Street and the Market Place
With its quaint old tower bell,
Coloured terraced houses,
There's The Doctors Pond as well.

Where children feed the ducks and geese
And men, cast their fishing lines,
While others stroll the pathways
Of the park, to pass their time.

There's some restaurants and a pub or two
And a club for only men,
Dating from the first world war,
And to the unreturned -
A cenotaph for them.

There's The Maltings, (once a brewery)
A small museum now takes it's place,
And since the thirteenth century
Saint Mary's Church, the town has graced.

Four hundred years or more,
The Clock House dates in time,
With stories of it hiding priests
And the martyr, Annie Line.

This piece of leafy, green old England,
Not known much for its fame,
A happy, pretty, country town
And Great Dunmow is its name.

Mother B

Mother B mother B
you gave birth to me
And you, were so gentle and kind.
You bathed me in oil,
I was dressed like a royal,
And nowhere was I left behind.

And you'd take me town
On the tram, if I frowned,
You'd buy me some sweets or a pie,
And I'd sit on your knee after lunch
And we'd be,
Counting the birds flying by.

And you'd visit your friends
At these times I would spend,
Looking at books or at play,
With the boy and his toys,
I really enjoyed, being with you
On your cleaning day.

Having meals at the table,
Made me etiquette able
"Show respect" you said, "be polite",
Use the fork on the left,
spoon in the middle,
And the knife is placed on the right

I remembered the rhymes
In the night at bedtime,
I kept them alive in my head.
You'd recite them to me,
Every night before sleep
As you tucked me up tight in my bed.

I can still hear your laughter
Though you suffered with asthma
Almost each day of your life,
You were born here from heaven
And six days out of seven
A hardworking mother, daughter, and wife.

You lived to old age
You were wise, a real sage,
But dementia in the end took its toll
I could only look on,
As you came upon
Your meeting, with your greater soul.

Aigburth

We'd all get together
On a Friday night,
Sometimes we'd squabble
And sometimes we'd fight,
Listen to chatter
Put the world to right,
On a Friday night in Aigburth

Some might have thought
We were crazy or daft,
The noise that we'd make
If someone slipped or made a gaff,
We had loads of fun,
And lots of laughs
On a Friday night in Aigburth .

Madge and Bertha
Grandma as well,
Joe and Clare,
You never could tell
Who'd turn up
And ring the bell,
On a Friday night in Aigburth.

Madeleine, Peter,
And Rosemary,
Paula, Elaine,
Denise and me
And Denny,
Sat together
On a small settee,
On a Friday night in Aigburth

The Cammack's would come
Barbara, Ed,
Arthur and Elsie
And what was said ?
Hiawatha, by Harry,
Which he often read
On a Friday night in Aigburth.

We'd all turn up
At sixty eight A,
Go the cast iron shore,
That's where we'd play,
On a hot summer night
Till close of day,
On a Friday night in Aigburth

Sometimes, Arthur
And brother Joe
Would get up on the floor
And give us a show,
Sing songs, tell jokes
That we didn't know,
On a Friday night in Aigburth.

Fun and laughs
And no TV
Games and stories
And here would be,
A gather of our family
On a Friday night in Aigburth.

The clock would tick
And the bell would chime,
Off home to bed
And a nursery rhyme,
Memories of
A really good time
On a Friday night in Aigburth.

Autumn

When Autumn comes
Then leaves must fall
For this is Nature's way,
Your Autumn came
Now we recall
The passing of your day.
In Nature's heart there burns a flame,
I know this flame will bring
Comfort to each one of us,
To you another spring.

Retirement

Old age and work retirement,
(It comes 'round pretty fast)
One day much like another
Recalling times of memories past.

No more rise at six a.m.
It's lie in every day,
No commute by bus or car,
No sights along the way.

No colleagues to do banter with
Or self worth at job well done,
No lifelong learning to pass on,
Just thoughts of days to come.

The aches and pains and medicines,
Replacement knee joints and false hips,
Influenza jabs and blood tests,
As old age tightens up its grip.

But youth still goes on drinking,
Smoking, staying late,
Having fun and like the ostrich
Head in sand to future fate.

And it's just the same old stories
Heard from them before,
Young hectic lives too busy
To heed the warnings anymore.

So remember when the time comes
That old age is there to stay,
Don't ignore it in your youthfulness
And don't forget to pray.

For it's us that you're replacing
You don't feel your growing old,
You don't see us disappearing
You can't see old age unfold.

A Family Holiday

The sun, the beach,
The fresh sea air,
A family holiday
In Cavalaire.
A seaside town
In South of France,
Happiness comes not
By chance.
We bathed, we swam,
We ate, we strolled,
Children played,
Refreshed our souls.
Building castles In the sand,
With buckets and spades
And children's hands.
Along the coast,
Out for the day,
We spent some time
In San Tropez.
Through the streets
And alleyways,
The quaint old shops,
Ice cream, cafes.
Down by the harbour,
Forget me not,
The millionaires
Aboard their yachts.
The onward journey
Through scenery

Of lush green vineyards,
To meet with friends in Italy.
(At Villa San Lorenzo)
Far from the city throng,
We wined and dined,
And sang some songs.
We ambled through the villages,
Montforte D'Alba, Dogliani,
Not forgetting old La Morra
In the region Piemonte.
We caught some fish and sunbathed,
We tasted local wine,
And by the pool lost track of day
And also track of time.
Helvetia duly beckoned,
On recollection I recall,
The streams, the lakes
And mountains tall,
The crisp blue sky,
The waterfalls,
The gentle breeze,
The valleys, trees
And good was time
So had by all.

Provence

Trees can talk, so can the sky
Green pastures speak of times gone by,
Mountains shout, yet we seldom hear
Natures voice, sweet to the ear.
Valleys deep, hamlets sit
High on the rocks atop the cliffs.
Winding roads, stops on the way
For quiet reflection at start of day.
Old man and dog on journey to
A village close, part of the view,
To him routine, this is his norm
His part of France, where he was born.
I wonder if his ears rejoice
At this, the sound of godly voice,
Coupled with an infants eye
Looking out as we pass by.
And listening to the morning song
Of larks and trees and valleys long,
Amid the hills of old Provence.
We stayed, and played, relaxed there once.

Little Arrow

When you little arrow
Are released through the air,
Take with you our guidance
And well may you fare,

Be kind and courageous
Try not to condemn,
The folly and failings
Of women and men.

Be brave little arrow
As you fly through the air,
Stay true to yourself
And always adhere,

To the words of the faithful,
The just and the wise,
Stay calm little arrow
As you move through the sky.

You'll soon reach your target
And there you should stay
And live out you life
In a meaningful way.

For you are the arrow,
Your parents the bow
Discover the archer,
No more you need know.

One In A Million

When you are fully grown my son
When you become a man,
There are things you'll need to know,
You'll need to have a plan.

No matter in whose company you be
Or where you are,
Take with you this advice
Rest assured you will go far.

Take care, be kind, be natural,
Invoke a sense of peace,
Strive to be yourself
Don't try too hard to please.

For when you please you'll feel content,
But when you don't, don't worry,
There are things you can't prevent
So don't be in a hurry.

Keep your temper in an argument,
Be sure to know your place,
Take time and care and choose your words
Then speak your mind with grace.

Nurture self respect,
Always be polite,
Get to know your limitations
Seek the truth of them in spite.

Employ imagination,
Be not it's employee,
Treat the same both loss and gain
And act unselfishly.

Remember that you're only one of millions
And what's more,
There's millions to come after you
And millions gone before.

Brown Eyed Girl

With eyes of brown and hair so fair,
When you were born I was there
It took nine months yet in a sec'
You were born (with the cord 'round your neck)

Inside I froze what could I do,
Your face was purple, turning blue,
And I felt pain deep inside,
With thoughts and prayer, no please don't die.

The nurse with scissors quickly cut,
The cord and then you were put,
In mother's arms first breath then cried
And we felt joy and good inside.

Back home with sister, brother too
And we took snaps of the three of you.
With tiny fingers, tiny feet
Our family now was complete.

I held you in my arms at times
And smile and sing you nursery rhymes.
Beautiful, fair haired, brown eyed girl,
Worth more than gold, diamonds pearl.

I stood back and watched you grow,
Through the high, through the low.
Through infancy and teenage years,
Through the laughs, the joy, the tears.

Yes watch you grow, yourself unfold,
Strong charactered, impulsive, bold,
From child to woman, to motherhood,
A sense of love and all was good.

Young Fair Child

Young fair child of Swiss descent,
As if by fate you were meant,
To come into his life,
Become his wife,
Bring love and joy and a sweet content.

Young fair child I tell you this
He saw in you a kind of bliss,
Temperance, patience,
Virtue true, he saw in you,
How could he miss ?

Young fair child from Switzerland,
We watched you both walk hand in hand,
Through Zurich's streets,
Through mountain side,
And each one's love could neither hide.

Young fair child of French, Swiss blood
Remember this - And believe you should,
This world was meant for such as you,
True and pure and all that's good.

I am There

When you need someone to talk to,
When you need a friendly ear,
I am there to listen
Each day throughout the year.

I am there to comfort you
If you feel the need to shout,
I am there to bare your pain,
To drive away the doubt.

I am there to bring you hope,
To wash away despair,
To help you laugh and live and love
And troubles help you share.

But first you must not blame yourself
And put in me your trust,
Let me be that person
And forgive my faults, you must.

Years

The years sincere
The laughs the tears
The highs the lows,
The joys the woes.
The days the nights,
The wrongs the rights.
The family homes,
The spends, the loans.
The weddings, births,
A wealth of worth.
The smiles, the joy,
The girls, the boy,
The kids to school,
The playing the fool.
The children's ills.
The cars, the frills.
The country walks,
The family talks.
The friends that stayed,
The hols away.
The working hard,
The games of cards.
The family pets,
The good it gets.
The fooling about,
The falling out .
The sharing of wine,
The good old times
The wages earned,

The lessons learned.
The parties, laughter
The looking after.
The mum's that reared us,
The care that shared us.
The heights, the depths,
The family deaths.
The fun, the fears,
The ageing years.
The ups the downs,
The lost, the found.
The buts the ifs,
The family tiffs,
The brave the bold,
The growing old.
The fun, the sorrow,
The new tomorrow.
The half full cup,
The making up.
The hugs, embraces,
The happy faces.
The something old,
The something new,
The family crew.

The Fifties

I can remember it's not long ago,
If you went for a walk along the Old Dock Road,
All day long the place was aglow
With workers, stevedores.

There were cobbled streets and tramway lines,
The night was lit by gas lamp lights
And overhead ran a railway line,
They called the dockers umbrella

We'd take the ferry to Wallasey
And I'd walk the prom' with my family,
We'd go to the fair at New Brighton
And paddle in the sea,
Well the Mersey River really.

One time at the fair when I was a kid,
I won a goldfish in a jar but from my hand it slid,
It fell in the gutter and got washed down the grid
And I cried all the way home.

Back home we'd play marbles in the street
And some kids had no shoes or socks on their feet,
But what made a hot summer day complete
Was a penny lolly-ice on a stick.

And we'd sit in the street bursting bubbles in the tar
We'd get covered in the stuff, then home to your ma'
She'd play bloody hell with her hands 'round a jar
Of Echo margarine.

And with pocket money I got from me dad,
I'd buy myself a 'lucky bag'
Or get two halfpenny chicks and three black jacks
And a piece of 'sticky lice'

There'd be my brother and me
And the kids next door,
And we'd often go down to the cast iron shore,
They made a film there once, starred Frankie Vaughn,
Called These Dangerous Years.

And we'd play all day in the streets and the park,
From early morning to nearly dark,
Skipping lifts on the back of a horse and cart,
Playing with peashooters and catapults.

On Friday nights in the old bathtub
In front of the fire give me back a scrub,
Then off to bed as snug as a bug
With dreams of cowboys and Indians .

Then on Saturday morning around about nine,
In me bed I'd be lyin' and a voice would cry out, "Any ol' iron"
And I'd listen to the noise his handcart made
As he pushed it down the jigger.

Once a month the priest would call
Father Darragh and Sister Paul
And I'd hide behind the door in the hall
If I hadn't been to church that Sunday.

Every year on Grand National day
Mrs. Harris would walk up the back yard and say,
"Is it a shilling to win or a tanner each way"
Cos she was the bookie's runner.

And now and then the tally man would come,
He'd knock on the door and say to me mum,
"If you need some cash I can loan you some"
But she always said,
"No thank you"

I can remember it's not long ago
Skipping ropes, re-al-ee-o
And Saturday matinees at The Cameo,
Hopscotch, rounders and kick the can.

No T.V. but the playing of cards,
Football, cricket in our back yard,
Times were tough but men were hard,
Back in the nineteen fifties.

These were the days just after the war,
When hearts were kind and hands were sore,
They say that were better off now
But I'm not so sure,
Times have changed haven't they?

*I hope you enjoyed
reading my mind !*

www.ingramcontent.com/pod-product-compliance
Lightning Source LLC
Chambersburg PA
CBHW051727040426
42447CB00008B/1003